Easter Story about Jesus

FOR LITTLE BOYS AND GIRLS

A Simplified Bible Storybook with Large Pictures
for Toddlers and Kids Ages 3-5

A GIFT FOR:

FROM:

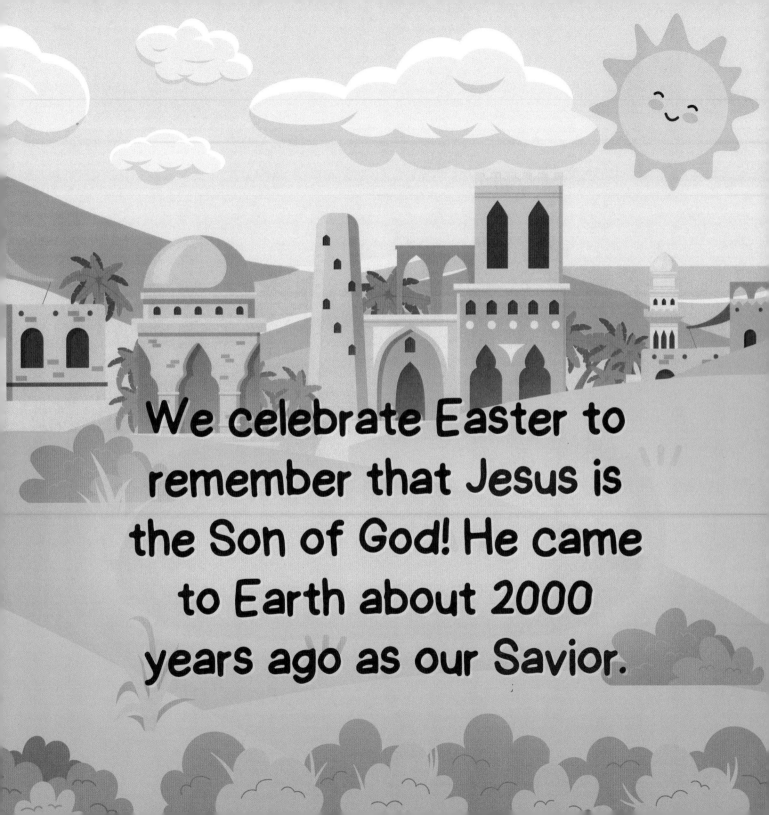

We celebrate Easter to remember that Jesus is the Son of God! He came to Earth about 2000 years ago as our Savior.

The baby JESUS was born in Bethlehem. ANGELS announced His birth, and SHEPHERDS were told to worship Him. Three WISE MEN from the East followed a star to find Him and bring Him gifts.

JESUS grew up and began teaching people about GOD. He healed sick people, fed thousands of hungry people with a small amount of food, and calmed dangerous storms. These MIRACLES show that Jesus is the Son of God.

Jesus and His disciples traveled to Jerusalem for the PASSOVER. There, Jesus rode into the city on a DONKEY while people waved PALM BRANCHES and shouted, "Hosanna! Hosanna!"

Jesus celebrated the Passover with His twelve disciples. During the LAST SUPPER, Jesus consecrated BREAD and WINE at the table.

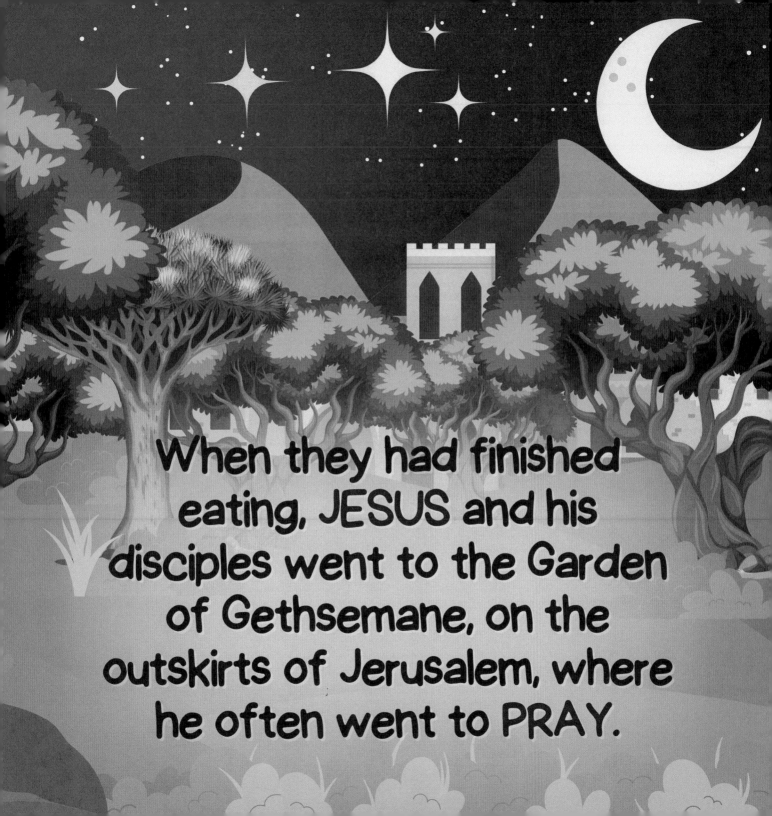

When they had finished eating, JESUS and his disciples went to the Garden of Gethsemane, on the outskirts of Jerusalem, where he often went to PRAY.

Even though JESUS had done nothing wrong, the religious LEADERS sent soldiers to arrest Him.

The soldiers forced JESUS to carry a heavy wooden CROSS up a hill. It was difficult to carry, and he fell several times. Finally, the soldiers put Jesus on the cross to die. His FRIENDS were very sad.

Three days after Jesus' death, some WOMEN came to see his tomb. They met an ANGEL who rolled away the stone and told them, "Jesus is not here. He has risen today!"

Jesus died, and after three days he came back to life. The WOMEN went to announce the news of the Resurrection to the disciples. Suddenly, JESUS met them. He smiled and said, "Go tell my brothers that I will see them in Galilee."

The DISCIPLES gathered in a small room. Suddenly, JESUS appeared to them! He asked them to touch his hands and feet, saying: "It is really me and I am ALIVE!"

The disciples were glad to see Jesus again. He told them, "Go and teach everyone about Me. Tell them everything you learned from Me. I will always BE WITH YOU!" Jesus blessed the disciples and then ascended to HEAVEN.

Happy Easter!

Dear child, you now know why we celebrate EASTER! Jesus died for our sins, but he came back to life after three days. God resurrected Jesus from the dead. Jesus is the SAVIOR of humanity, and one day He will RETURN again. Jesus loves all people very much and calls us to love everyone too!

We'd like to know what you think!

We'd be super grateful if you could spare a few minutes to leave us a review! Thank you for choosing our books!

ASIN: B0BKS93RHN

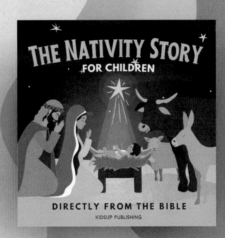

ASIN: B0BMDC7C6Q

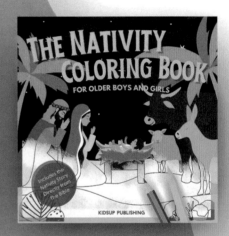

ASIN: B0BN277C2Z

If you enjoyed this story, please check out our other popular books.

Made in the USA
Las Vegas, NV
09 March 2024

86857603R00019